COOKING CHEMISTRY
HOW DOES ICE CREAM FREEZE?

by Tracy Vonder Brink

pogo

Ideas for Parents and Teachers

Pogo Books let children practice reading informational text while introducing them to nonfiction features such as headings, labels, sidebars, maps, and diagrams, as well as a table of contents, glossary, and index.

Carefully leveled text with a strong photo match offers early fluent readers the support they need to succeed.

Before Reading

- "Walk" through the book and point out the various nonfiction features. Ask the student what purpose each feature serves.
- Look at the glossary together. Read and discuss the words.

During Reading

- Have the child read the book independently.
- Invite them to list questions that arise from reading.

After Reading

- Discuss the child's questions. Talk about how they might find answers to those questions.
- Prompt the child to think more. Ask: Have you ever thought about how ice cream freezes? What questions about ice cream do you have?

Pogo Books are published by Jump!
3500 American Blvd W, Suite 150
Bloomington, MN 55431
www.jumplibrary.com

Copyright © 2026 Jump! International copyright reserved in all countries. No part of this book may be reproduced in any form without written permission from the publisher.

Jump! is a division of FlutterBee Education Group.

Library of Congress Cataloging-in-Publication Data is available at www.loc.gov or upon request from the publisher.

ISBN: 979-8-89213-837-6 (hardcover)
ISBN: 979-8-89213-838-3 (paperback)
ISBN: 979-8-89213-839-0 (ebook)

Editor: Katie Chanez
Designer: Anna Peterson

Photo Credits: fcafotodigital/iStock, cover; subjug/iStock, 1, 4; Valentina Proskurina/Shutterstock, 3; Candice Bell/iStock, 5; PawelG Photo/Shutterstock, 6; TayaJohnston/Shutterstock, 7; Amelia Fox/Shutterstock, 8-9; AlessandroZocc/Shutterstock, 10-11; Susanne Kischnick/Alamy, 12-13; ZoranMilisavljevic83/iStock, 14-15; MaraZe/Shutterstock, 16-17; Diane Labombarbe/iStock, 18 (recipe card); Noel V. Baebler/Shutterstock, 18 (vanilla); Artiom Photo/Shutterstock, 18 (milk); Katie Chanez, 19, 20 (top), 21; Anna Peterson, 20 (bottom); Su Nitram/iStock, 23.

Printed in the United States of America at Corporate Graphics in North Mankato, Minnesota.

TABLE OF CONTENTS

CHAPTER 1
Ice Cream Basics.....................4

CHAPTER 2
Ice Cream Science....................6

CHAPTER 3
Let's Make Ice Cream!................18

ACTIVITIES & TOOLS
Try This!............................22
Glossary............................23
Index...............................24
To Learn More.......................24

CHAPTER 1

ICE CREAM BASICS

Ice cream is a cold and creamy treat. It comes in many **flavors**.

4 CHAPTER 1

Ice cream is made by mixing milk, sugar, and cream. The mixture is put into a machine. It **churns** and **freezes**. Other **ingredients** like chocolate or strawberries can be added.

CHAPTER 1

CHAPTER 2
ICE CREAM SCIENCE

How does ice cream freeze? Milk and cream both have water. The ice cream machine is cold. It freezes part of the water. More water **molecules** attach to the frozen bits. They form ice **crystals**.

ice crystals

cream

Cream has fat in it. Fat molecules mix with the ice crystals. This stops the ice crystals from sticking together. Sugar also keeps the ice crystals apart. This keeps them small.

CHAPTER 2

The size of the crystals changes how ice cream feels in your mouth. Your tongue does not notice tiny crystals. This makes the ice cream feel smooth. Large crystals make ice cream feel rough.

An ice cream machine has **paddles**. These churn the ingredients as they freeze. This creates air bubbles. The bubbles act like cushions between the crystals. This makes the ice cream soft.

paddle

TAKE A LOOK!

How is ice cream made? Take a look!

1 Water in milk and cream freezes. Ice crystals form.

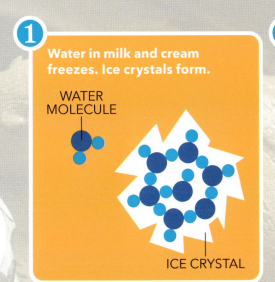

2 Fat and sugar keep them from sticking together.

3 The ice cream is churned. Air bubbles make it smooth and creamy.

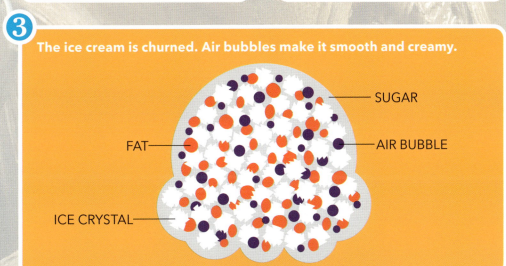

CHAPTER 2 11

old ice cream machine

The first ice cream machines were churned by hand. The mixture went into a container surrounded by ice and salt. The salt lowered the **melting point** of the ice. This helped the ice stay frozen longer. A handle turned the paddles. The ice cream froze.

Now ice cream machines have a freezer built in. The ice cream freezes fast.

DID YOU KNOW?

Some ice cream is made by pouring liquid **nitrogen** over the mixture. It is about –320 degrees Fahrenheit (–196 degrees Celsius). The ice cream freezes in about one minute!

CHAPTER 2   13

The ice cream is taken out of the machine. Sometimes more ingredients are added. These can include nuts or candy pieces. **Syrups** like chocolate and caramel can be added, too.

DID YOU KNOW?

In 2024, the top ice cream flavors in the United States were:
- vanilla
- chocolate
- strawberry
- butter pecan
- cookie dough

CHAPTER 2

Then ice cream is put into a freezer. It gets even colder. This makes it **firm**. It is ready to scoop. Yum!

DID YOU KNOW?

Soft serve is a type of ice cream. It has more air in it than other types of ice cream. The extra air keeps it soft.

CHAPTER 2

CHAPTER 3

LET'S MAKE ICE CREAM!

Let's make ice cream in a bag! Gather your ingredients and kitchen tools.

ICE CREAM IN A BAG

INGREDIENTS
- ½ cup (118 milliliters) milk
- ½ cup (118 mL) heavy whipping cream
- 2 tablespoons (21 grams) sugar
- ½ teaspoon (2.5 mL) of vanilla or 1 tablespoon (15 mL) chocolate syrup
- ½ cup (250 g) rock salt
- ice

KITCHEN TOOLS
- small bowl
- 1 gallon freezer bag
- 1 quart freezer bag
- small towel

START WITH THESE STEPS:

1

Mix the milk, heavy whipping cream, sugar, and vanilla or chocolate syrup in a bowl.

2

Pour the mixture into the quart bag. Seal it tightly.

CHAPTER 3

3

Fill the gallon bag half full with ice. Put the bag with the mixture inside the gallon bag. Make sure it sits on the ice.

4

Fill the gallon bag with ice and add the salt. Seal the large bag tightly. Make sure the ice is all around the smaller bag. Wrap a towel around the bag.

5

Shake the bag for 5 to 10 minutes. You will feel the mixture start to get solid.

6

Stop shaking when it feels thick. Remove the ice cream from the small bag. Enjoy!

CHAPTER 3　21

ACTIVITIES & TOOLS

TRY THIS!

MAKE INDIAN ICE CREAM

Not all ice creams are churned. Find out how an ice cream from India, called kulfi, is made with this fun activity!

What You Need:
- 1 cup (237 mL) sweetened condensed milk
- ½ cup (118 mL) heavy whipping cream
- ½ cup (118 mL) milk
- 1 teaspoon (2 g) ground cardamom
- ¼ cup (25 g) chopped pistachios (optional)
- bowl
- 4 to 6 small paper cups
- 4 to 6 Popsicle sticks
- plastic wrap or wax paper
- rubber bands

❶ Put the ingredients in the bowl. Mix.

❷ Pour the mixture evenly into the paper cups.

❸ Cover the cups with plastic wrap or wax paper. Use rubber bands to hold it in place.

❹ Poke one Popsicle stick into each cup through the plastic wrap or wax paper.

❺ Freeze for about six hours. Then enjoy!

GLOSSARY

churns: Stirs and moves a substance.

crystals: Substances that form patterns of many flat surfaces when solid.

firm: Solid.

flavors: Tastes.

freezes: Turns to ice at a very low temperature.

ingredients: Items used to make something.

melting point: The temperature at which a substance goes from solid to liquid.

molecules: The smallest units that chemicals can be divided into.

nitrogen: A colorless, odorless gas that makes up most of Earth's atmosphere.

paddles: Flat tools used for stirring or mixing.

syrups: Thick, sweet liquids made by boiling sugar and water, usually with flavoring.

ACTIVITIES & TOOLS 23

INDEX

chocolate 5, 14, 18, 19
churns 5, 10, 11, 13
cream 5, 6, 7, 11, 18, 19
crystals 6, 7, 9, 10, 11
fat 7, 11
flavors 4, 14
freezes 5, 6, 10, 11, 13, 17
liquid nitrogen 13
machine 5, 6, 10, 13, 14

melting point 13
milk 5, 6, 11, 18, 19
paddles 10, 13
salt 13, 18, 20
soft serve 17
sugar 5, 7, 11, 18, 19
syrups 14, 18, 19
vanilla 14, 18, 19
water 6, 11

TO LEARN MORE

Finding more information is as easy as 1, 2, 3.
1. Go to www.factsurfer.com
2. Enter "icecream" into the search box.
3. Choose your book to see a list of websites.

24 ACTIVITIES & TOOLS